ANNE GEDDES ™

ISBN 0-7683-2023-2

© Anne Geddes 1997

Published in 1997 by Photogenique Publishers (a division of Hodder Moa Beckett)
Studio 3.16, Axis Building, 1 Cleveland Road, Parnell
Auckland, New Zealand

First USA edition published in 1997 by Cedco Publishing Company,
100 Pelican Way, San Rafael, CA 94901

Designed by Francis Young
Produced by Kel Geddes
Color separations by Image Centre

Printed through Midas Printing Limited, Hong Kong

Please write to us for a FREE FULL COLOR catalog of our fine Anne Geddes
calendars and books, Cedco Publishing Company, 100 Pelican Way.,
San Rafael, CA 94901.
Visit our website : www.cedco.com

ANNE GEDDES

SHAPES

Cedco

SQUARE

OVAL

RECTANGLE

HEART

SPIRAL

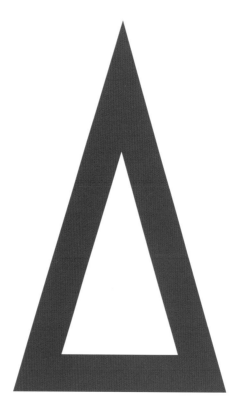

TRIANGLE

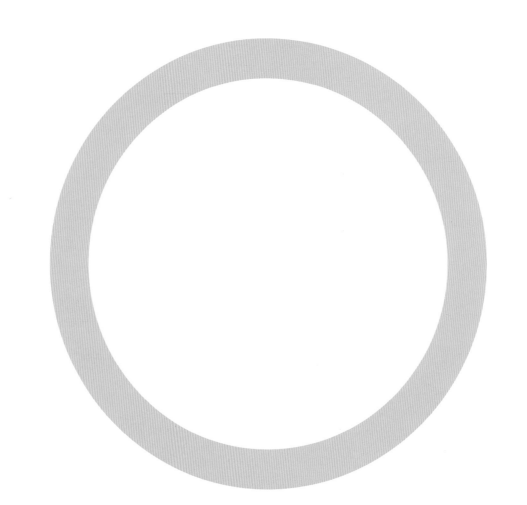

CIRCLE

HALF-CIRCLE

HEXAGON

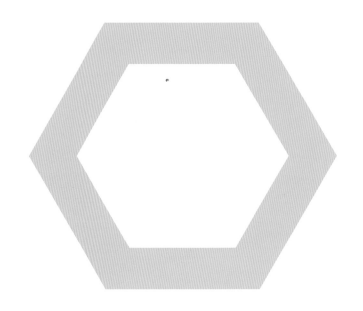

STAR

HOW MANY CORNERS DOES...

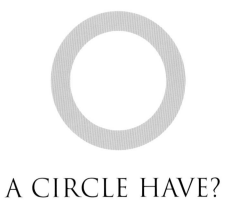

A CIRCLE HAVE?

A HALF-CIRCLE?

A HEART?

AN OVAL?

A RECTANGLE?

A STAR?

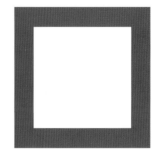

A SQUARE?

A SPIRAL?

A TRIANGLE?

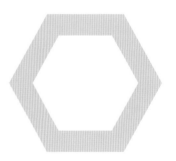

AND A HEXAGON?

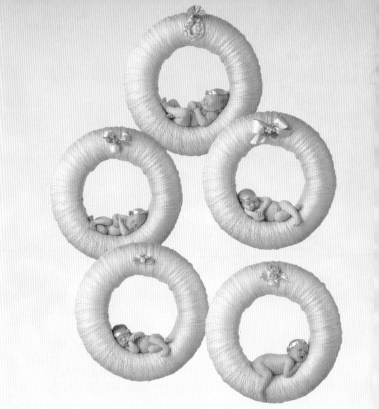

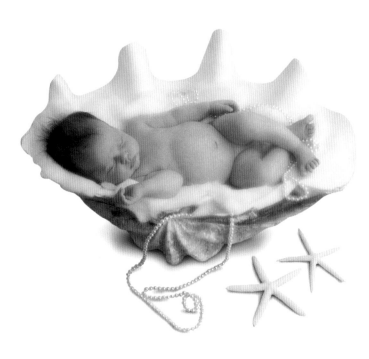

SHAPES CAN YOU FIND?

HOW MANY DIFFERENT SHAPES CAN YOU FIND IN YOUR ROOM?